BRITISH SUPERCARS

MCLAREN • ASTON MARTIN • JAGUAR

Paul Mason

PowerKiDS
press™

Published in 2019 by The Rosen
Publishing Group, Inc.
29 East 21st Street, New York, NY 10010

Cataloging-in-Publication Data

Names: Mason, Paul.

Title: British supercars: McLaren, Aston
Martin, Jaguar / Paul Mason.

Description: New York : PowerKids Press,
2019. | Series: Supercars | Includes glossary
and index.

Identifiers: LCCN ISBN 9781538338834 (pbk.)
| ISBN 9781538338827 (library bound) | ISBN
9781538338841 (6 pack)

Subjects: LCSH: Sports cars--Juvenile
literature. | Automobiles, Racing--Juvenile
literature.

Classification: LCC TL236.M29 2019 | DDC
629.222--dc23

Copyright © 2019 Franklin Watts,
a division of Hachette Children's Group

Executive editor: Adrian Cole
Series designer: Mayer Media
Design manager: Peter Scoulding
Picture researcher: Diana Morris

Picture Credits:

Alizada Studios/Shutterstock: 4-5c, 31b.
Ascari: 7c, 7t. Aston Martin: back cover,
1b, 3c, 12-13c, 13t, 8t, 10-11, 13t, 28t. BAC:
28c. Pieter Beens/Shutterstock. 27t. Columbia/
EON/Da/REX/Shutterstock: 17t. Mike Dodd/
McLaren Automotive: 24-25c. Jaguar: front
cover t, 28b, 29t. Sergey Kohl/Shutterstock:
5t. Radoslaw Lecyk/Shutterstock: 30cr. Lotus
Cars: 3t, 3b, 18-19t, 19b, 20-21c, 21t. Magic
Car Pics/REX/Shutterstock: 5b. McLaren
Automotive: front cover b, 22-23b, 25b, 29cr,
29cl, 32. Noble Cars: 26-27c. Rachel Palmer/
Aston Martin: 8-9b. Sotheby's: 30cl. Maskim

Toome/Shutterstock: 15t. TVR: 29b.
Miro Vrlik Photography/Shutterstock: 14-15c.
CC Wikimedia: 30t, 30bl,30br. Vande Wolf
Images/Dreamstime: 1t, 16-17. Aleksandr
Zavatskiy/Dreamstime: 23c.

Kevlar® is a registered trademark of
E. I. du Pont de Nemours and Company

Manufactured in the United States of America

CPSIA Compliance Information: Batch
CSPK18: For Further Information contact Ros-
en Publishing, New York, New York at 1-800-
237-9932.

Contents

Words highlighted in **bold** can be found in the glossary

BUILDING CLASSIC SUPERCARS

Ever since cars were invented in the late 1800s, British companies have been building high-performance, expensive, sometimes impractical cars. But in 1961, Jaguar released a car that became probably the world's most famous fast car: the Jaguar E-Type.

THE BIG THREE

Jaguar still makes supercars. So do two other big British companies: Aston Martin and McLaren. McLaren is famous for producing cars that use Formula 1 technology on the road. Aston Martin and Jaguar are famous for GT, or 'Grand Tourer', models. These are designed to cover long distances in comfort – but very, very quickly.

Several other British companies make high-performance cars. Some, like Ascari, make true supercars, while companies such as Lotus make cars that can be adapted for racing. Others, like TVR, have struggled to stay in business.

What's it like to ~~drive?~~ look at?

The most beautiful car in the world.

– Enzo Ferrari (yes, THAT Enzo, the one who founded Ferrari) speaking about the Jaguar E-Type

Each wheel has its own independent suspension system

Leather race-car-style **bucket seats** in early E-Types were later replaced by more comfortable seats

The Jaguar E-Type was the first British supercar. It was based on the D-Type racing car, which won the Le Mans 24-hour endurance race in 1955, 1956, and 1957.

Disc brakes on all four wheels were race car technology in 1961

Price Tag...

Start saving! The most expensive E-Types are the Series 1 Lightweights. Only 12 were ever made, and in 2015 one of them was sold for nearly $8 million. Even an "ordinary" Series 1 costs more than most houses.

E-TYPE TIMELINE

1961 — Jaguar E-Type appears at the Geneva Motor Show. Demand for test drives is so high that a second car is driven from the Jaguar factory in Coventry to Geneva in one night.

1964 — Engine size is increased to 4200 cc

1968 — Series 2 E-Type is released, with many changes to fit in with US safety regulations

1971 — Series 3 E-Type, with a 5300 cc V12 engine; production stops in 1975

The Aston Martin DB4, launched in 1958, was the quickest production car of its time.

0–60 MPH

7 seconds

MAX POWER

198 kW

(266 **bhp**) @ 5,500 rpm

MAX **TORQUE**

325 Nm

(240 ft/lb) @ 4,000 rpm

JUST WHAT *IS* A SUPERCAR?

There is no exact definition of what makes a supercar. But most supercars share some of these features:

- Expensive
- Made in small numbers
- High-performance in every area of their design
- Very fast, and probably very light
- Tricky to drive
- Not ideal for daily driving

Four-speed manual gearbox has no **synchromesh** on first gear – which makes using first and second gear a real challenge

Glass-covered headlights featured on early E-Types

The 1958 TVR Grantura had a fiberglass body, and helped to launch the TVR company.

Max RPM:

not known

Engine:

3800 cc **inline 6**

Weight:

2,900 lbs

Fuel use per 60 miles (estimated):

13.3 liters

CO2:

not known

Gearbox:

4-speed **manual**

Drive:

rear wheels

Main body:

steel

Frame:

steel

Braking:

steel

KZ1

Ascari is named after Alberto Ascari, an Italian racing driver. He was the first person ever to win the Formula 1 World Championship more than once. You would expect a car from a company like that to be fast – and the KZ1 is definitely fast.

The owner of Ascari is a rich Dutch businessman named Klaas Zwart. He was once described as "the biggest **petrolhead** in the world." Zwart designed the KZ1 to be as simple and lightweight as possible, without the electronic driver aids used in many supercars. If you start to skid in a KZ1, the car's computer will not help you!

THE KZ1-R
Ascari also produces a racing version of the KZ1, the KZ1-R. The inside is almost completely stripped out. There are no electric windows, no comfortable seats (just lightweight carbon fiber ones), no leather trim and no carpets. But, the KZ1-R is so lightweight that it speeds off as quickly as a Lamborghini Murcielago LP640.

THE ASCARI RACE RESORT
In 2002, Ascari opened its own racetrack in southern Spain. Buying a KZ1 gives you the right to use the 5.5-km circuit, and drivers can also try the Ascari LMP900 racing car.

Rear **spoiler** automatically comes up at 50 mph, giving the back tires extra grip

Side vents channel air to the engine, cooling it and providing oxygen. The oxygen is needed so the engine can burn vast amounts of fuel.

Engine is based on a BMW M5's, but with most parts changed or adapted. The KZ1 has almost 30 percent more power.

What's it like to drive?
One of the finest-handling supercars of this or any generation. No Ferrari made today steers as well as this, no Porsche can match its blend of ride and refinement.

– review on *autocar.co.uk*

KZ1 TIMELINE

2000	2004	2005

Ascari starts taking orders for the KZ1

Ascari first reveals the KZ1 concept car

The first KZ1s are delivered; the KZ1-R is announced

Price Tag...

When it was launched in 2005, the KZ1 cost a minimum of $300,000, or more if you added extras. Only a few have ever been made, and these cars very rarely come up for sale used.

TOP SPEED

200 mph

(322 km/h)

0–60 MPH

3.9 seconds

MAX POWER

373 kW

(500 bhp) @ 7,000 rpm

MAX TORQUE

499 Nm

(368 ft/lb) @ 4,500 rpm

The KZ1-R* is the race car version of the design. It is lighter and more powerful than the normal car — but not as comfortable.

Entire body apart from doors and bumpers is made of lightweight carbon fiber

OU04 VOG

Max RPM:

7,250

Engine:

4941 cc V8

Weight:

2,810 lbs

Fuel use per 60 miles:

not known

CO2:

not known

Gearbox:

6-speed manual

Drive:

rear wheels

Main body:

carbon fiber

Frame:

carbon fiber

Braking:

steel

NAME: Alberto Ascari
LIVED: 1918–55
FAMOUS AS: Racing driver

Ascari started as a motorbike racer before switching to cars. In 1952 he won the Formula 1 World Championship driving a Ferrari. He won a second championship, again in a Ferrari, in 1953. As an Italian driving an Italian car, Ascari became a national hero.

* The 'R' stands for Rebel.

VANTAGE GT12

The GT12 is what you get when you take "the most ferocious Aston Martin ever produced", and make it MORE ferocious!

Factory: Gaydon, Warwickshire

The GT12 is based on a V12 Vantage S. The Vantage S comes with a monstrous V12 engine, but is also Aston Martin's lightest car. But Aston decided it was not light enough. They shaved 220 lbs off the weight – which is the same as telling a heavy passenger to get out and walk. They made it lower and wider than any other Vantage. And they gave it different **aerodynamics**, with a bigger front **splitter** and a special rear **wing**.

The GT12 is very different from many supercars. In a Gumpert Apollo Enraged, for example, the noise of the engine is practically deafening – some drivers wear earplugs while driving one! The Vantage S is amazingly quiet by comparison. Almost no road noise reaches the driver – just the noise of the engine and exhaust roaring and crackling.

The GT12 features an upgraded Vantage engine, with lightweight magnesium parts.

Price Tag...

Only 100 GT12s were ever made, and they were all sold long ago. Buying one would have cost you $330,000 – which is about $160,000 more than a "standard" V12 Vantage S.

Much of the GT12's frame and **bodywork** is stuck together using glue

Carbon-fiber front splitter and rear wing improve aerodynamics

GT12

VANTAGE GT12 TIMELINE

2005 — The first Vantage is released

2013 — V12 Vantage S, lighter and more powerful than any previous Vantage

2015 — Aston Martin announces they will make 100 Vantage GT12s, a track-influenced version of the V12 Vantage S

What's it like to drive?

*A wonderful, characterful machine… That monstrous engine (and its soundtrack) dominates proceedings but dig deeper and you'll find brakes and **chassis** to match.*

– review on *carmagazine.co.uk*

TOP SPEED

205 mph
(330 km/h)

0–60 MPH

3.5 seconds

MAX POWER

441 kW
(592 bhp) @ 7,000 rpm

MAX TORQUE

625 Nm
(461 lb/ft) @ 5,500 rpm

Engine is front-mid mounted: in front of the driver, but behind the front wheels

Separate suspension system for each wheel

 Max RPM:
not known

 Engine:
5935 cc V12

 Weight:
3,450 lbs

Fuel use per 60 miles:
14.3 liters

 CO2:
323 g/km

 Gearbox:
7-speed automatic

 Drive:
rear wheels

 Main body:
carbon fiber

 Frame:
aluminum

 Braking:
carbon-ceramic

ASTON MARTIN
V12 ZAGATO

"Zagato" is a name Aston Martin gives cars it makes with the help of the Zagato factory in Italy. And Italy, as every car fan knows, is where supercars originally came from.*

Factory: Gaydon, Warwickshire

ZAGATO TIMELINE

1960	1986	2002	2012	2016
DB4 GT Zagato is released	V8 Vantage Zagato, the first of three Zagatos based on the Vanquish model	DB7 Vantage Zagato	V12 Vantage Zagato is released for sale	
			Release of 99 Vanquish V12 Zagatos	

THE FIRST ZAGATO

The first Zagato was the DB4 GT Zagato — one of the rarest cars Aston Martin ever built: only 19 were made. When it was released in 1960 it cost $7,200. This was a lot of money at the time, but today you could sell one for several million dollars!

THE V12 ZAGATO

The V12 Zagato was built to celebrate 50 years of the two companies working together. It is a more powerful, lighter version of an Aston Martin Vantage. The outside panels are all handmade using a combination of aluminum and carbon fiber for lightness. Its 5935 cc V12 engine spits the Vantage Zagato to 60 mph in about 4 seconds. This is an amazing speed for a luxury car that can be driven hundreds of miles in complete comfort.

Front splitter channels air to improve the Zagato's aerodynamics

"Sport" button on dashboard makes the engine respond more quickly and the exhaust more noisy

Huge front grille allows cooling air to flow into the engine space

*Most people think the Lamborghini Miura, which appeared in 1966, was the first supercar.

Price Tag...

If you want a new one, you're out of luck. Only 150 of them were made and they were all quickly sold. The basic car cost about $432,500 plus tax.

What's it like to drive?

Putting such a big engine in such a small car makes it an absolute hooligan to drive … whether you're gazing at it on your driveway or pelting across the countryside, you'll be grinning away madly as it gets your adrenaline pumping.

– review on autoexpress.com

NAME: Ugo Zagato
LIVED: 1890–1968
FAMOUS AS: Founder of Zagato **coachworks**

As a teenager, Zagato moved from Italy to Germany to work in a coachworks. He later returned to Italy, and during World War I worked building lightweight aircraft. When the war ended, Zagato began building lightweight racing car bodies for the Alfa Romeo racing team. Over the years since, Zagato's company has built special cars for Alfa Romeo, Jaguar, Spyker, Lamborghini, Ferrari and Aston Martin.

TOP SPEED
190 mph
(305 km/h)

0–60 MPH
42 seconds

MAX POWER
380 kW
(510 bhp) @ 6,500 rpm

MAX TORQUE
570 Nm
(420lb/ft) @ 5,750 rpm

Max RPM:
not known

Engine:
5935 cc V12 non-turbo

Weight:
3,700 lbs

Fuel use per 60 miles:
14.3 liters

CO2:
388 g/km

Gearbox:
6-speed manual

Drive:
rear wheels

Main body:
carbon fiber and aluminum

Frame:
alloy

Braking:
carbon-ceramic

Fixed rear wing adds **downforce**, giving the rear wheels better grip

ASTON MARTIN
DB11

Any car that comes fitted with "launch control" has to be good!
That's what Formula 1 cars have – space rockets, too.
And so does the Aston Martin DB11.

Factory: Gaydon, Warwickshire

BETTER THAN 007

This is the car that James Bond drove in *Spectre* – but better! Bond's car was a DB10, which Aston Martin built specially for the film. The DB10 was actually a **tricked-out** version of the DB9. Only two show-car DB10s were built. In 2016 one of them was sold at an auction for about $3.1 million.

The DB11 is the replacement for the DB9. It is one of the first modern Aston Martins to use turbo chargers. These whoosh extra air into the engine, feeding it more oxygen. The extra oxygen is used to burn more fuel, creating more power.

What's it like to drive?

The V12 howls that pure, complex tone and throttle response is excellent … it massively out punches the [DB9's] engine on corner exits and gives the rear tires a really hard time.

– review of a prototype DB11 on *evo.co.uk*

DB11 TIMELINE

1963			1994	2004	2016

The DB5 is released. A year later a gadget-filled version (with an ejector passenger seat, machine guns in the front bumpers, and a bulletproof rear panel!) appears in the James Bond film *Goldfinger*. The DB5 soon becomes many Bond fans' dream car.

DB7, the first modern DB-model car. Two racing versions are built; despite being stripped down racing cars, they have leather interiors because Aston Martin wants them to be "gentleman racers."

The first DB9s are released for sale. The DB9 is the last DB with a non-turbo engine.

The DB11 goes on sale at the end of the year

"Gills" on the side release air from the wheel arch, improving front-wheel grip and keeping the brakes cool.

The DB11 is a 2+2, which means there is just enough room for two small (or very scrunched-up) passengers in the back

Above 96 mph, a rear spoiler is automatically activated

Air is channeled through the body. It is released from slots in the trunk lid, improving aerodynamics.

Suspension can be set to GT, Sport and Sport+ modes. These are for rough roads; smooth, fast roads; or racetracks.

Price Tag...

Prices start around $202,900 for the cheapest DB11, but adding extras means most cars will actually cost more.

Max RPM:
7,000

Engine:
5200 cc   twin-turbo V12

Weight:
3,900 lbs

Fuel use per 60 miles:
11.8 liters (est.)

CO2:
270 g/km (est.)

Gearbox:
8-speed automatic

Drive:
rear wheels

Main body:
aluminum

Frame:
carbon fiber

Braking:
carbon-ceramic

FROM V12 TO INLINE 6
When the engine's whole power is not needed, one side of the V12 engine shuts down completely.

The engine becomes an inline 6, which reduces the amount of fuel the car uses and the amount of pollution it creates.

JAGUAR
F-TYPE SVR

When it went on sale in 2016, the F-Type SVR became the fastest production car Jaguar had ever made. This 200 mph rocket ship is part of a long line of fast Jaguars that goes back to the E-Type (see pages 4–5).

Factory: Birmingham, West Midlands

Jaguar's F-Type appeared in 2013. It was the company's first 2-seater sports car since the E-Type. The SVR version of the F-Type turns the dial up to "supercar." It is lighter, more powerful, and faster than any other road-going Jaguar.

SPECIAL VEHICLE OPERATIONS

The F-Type SVR was designed by Jaguar's brilliantly named "Special Vehicle Operations" team. This unit makes the most extreme Jaguars possible. The F-Type SVR (which is short for Special Vehicle Race), with its wider front end for enhanced aerodynamics and titanium exhaust, is the first Jaguar to be souped up by SVO.

Price Tag...

It will cost you at least $145,000. However, if you want to add extras such as carbon-ceramic brakes, black wheels, and carbon-fiber extras, the bill will be thousands more. Even the umbrella holder costs extra — and it doesn't even include an umbrella!

The carbon-fiber rear wing automatically lifts to improve grip at 70 mph (or when the driver puts the SVR into "Dynamic" driving mode). It increases downforce by 15 percent.

Lightweight alloy wheels

Titanium exhaust is lighter and sounds different from the standard F-Type exhaust

Air flows through the engine bay, under the car's smooth floor and out through the rear splitter

F-TYPE SVR TIMELINE

1961	1975	2013	2016
Jaguar E-Type is released, and immediately becomes a sensation around the world	Jaguar stops production of the E-Type	F-Type is released for sale	SVR model takes the F-Type into supercar territory

TOP SPEED

200 mph
(322 km/h)

0–60 MPH

3.7 seconds

MAX POWER

423 kW
(567 bhp) @ 6,500 rpm

MAX TORQUE

700 Nm
(516 lb/ft) @ 3,500 rpm

As well as a coupe, the SVR comes in a slightly more expensive convertible version. The convertible is not quite as fast, but some people think it looks even cooler than the coupe version!

What's it like to drive?

The F-Type's signature scream [sounds] like an angry King Kong thumping his chest at several thousand beats per minute. It's an appropriate soundtrack for Jaguar's fastest-ever production car.

– review on *caranddriver.com*

Vents in the front wings release air from the wheel arches, making the SVR more aerodynamic

 Max RPM:
6,750

 Engine:
5000 cc   supercharged V8

 Weight:
3,760 lbs

 Fuel use per 60 miles:
11 liters

 CO2:
269 g/km

 Gearbox:
8-speed automatic

 Drive:
all 4 wheels

 Main body:
aluminum

Frame:
aluminum

 Braking:
steel

NAME: Norman Dewis
LIVED: 1920–present
FAMOUS AS: Chief test driver for Jaguar, 1952–1985

Dewis is most famous for an overnight drive between Coventry, England, and Geneva, Switzerland, in 1961. The new E-Type was so popular at the Geneva Motor Show that a second car was needed the next day, so Dewis drove it from the Jaguar factory in Coventry to Geneva in 13 hours. When the motor show *Top Gear* tried to do the same thing in an F-Type SVR in 2016, they could not manage it. Dewis got there faster 55 years before!

JAGUAR
C-X75

When you take the company that makes the F-Type SVR, and add it together with the Williams Formula 1 team, what do you get? The Jaguar C-X75, that's what.

Factories: Birmingham, West Midlands and Wantage, Oxfordshire

THE PHEV SUPERCAR

PHEV stands for Plug-in Hybrid Electric Vehicle. PHEV cars get some of their power from a gas engine and some from an electric battery. They are not unusual: most big car companies make at least one. Not many can go 200 mph, though!

As well as electric power, the C-X75 uses a little 1600 cc engine inspired by Formula 1 cars. (The Williams F1 team helped Jaguar develop the C-X75.) The engine is supercharged until it reaches 5,500 rpm, as supercharging works best at low rpm. Then it switches to being turbocharged, as this works better once the engine is working faster.

MOVIE-STAR CAR

The C-X75 is an A-list movie star car. It's featured in the James Bond movie *Spectre*, racing through the streets of Rome alongside an Aston Martin DB10.

Battery pack behind the driver can be charged by being plugged in

Exhaust noise can be controlled by the driver, who can open or close flaps in the exhaust to change the noise

Grip is increased by the way air flows under the car and out the back. Gases flowing from the exhausts are also used to increase grip.

What's it like to drive?

*The shriek of the **supercharger** builds and builds until … 5,500 rpm [when] it's only the turbo forcing air through the engine … then the deep snarl and growl of the exhausts really takes over and starts to deafen you.*

– review on *carmagazine.co.uk*

Price Tag…

It's not going to happen. In 2010, Jaguar originally built five C-X75s, none of which went on sale. A year later they said 250 would be built and sold – but then in 2012 announced that a shortage of likely buyers meant the C-X75 would not yet be released.

C-X75 TIMELINE

2010	2011	2012	2015

A specially built C-X75 races through the streets of Rome in the Bond movie *Spectre*

Jaguar decides not to offer the C-X75 for sale, but carries on working on the car

Jet power is dropped in favor of a small, Formula 1 type gas engine

Jaguar shows off a jet-powered C-X75 at the Paris Motor Show

A C-X75 with headlights blazing as it chases an Aston Martin DB10 in the movie Spectre.

TOP SPEED

200 mph
(322 km/h)

0–60 MPH

3.4 seconds

MAX POWER

634 kW
(850+ bhp) @ 9,700 rpm

MAX TORQUE

1000 Nm
(738 lb/ft) @ 3,000 rpm

Engine fitted with an ECO **stop-start system**

When the brakes are used, the energy of the braking force is stored, then used to power the electric motors (like a Formula 1 car's **KERS** system)

Front grille and brake-cooling vents open only when needed. When they are closed, the C-X75 is more aerodynamic.

Gear shifts can be fully automatic, or controlled by the driver using steering-wheel paddles

*zero on electric power

Max RPM:
10,200

Engine:
1600 cc — inline 4 turbo supercharged; 2 electric motors

Weight:
3,000 lbs

Fuel use per 60 miles:
9.6 liters

CO2:
not known*

Gearbox:
7-speed

Drive:
all 4 wheels

Main body:
carbon fiber

Frame:
carbon-fiber **monocoque**

Braking:
carbon-ceramic

LOTUS
EXIGE 360 CUP

Factory: Hethel, Norfolk

The Exige is a tiny, lightweight, supercharged bundle of fun. Compared to massive-engined supercars like the Lamborghini Aventador, the Exige is not very powerful. But the car has such a simple design, and weighs so little, that it is super-exciting to drive.

WEIGHT VS PERFORMANCE

All designers of fast cars have to make a decision: weight vs performance. For example, a small engine is lighter than a big one – but the big one is more powerful. A manual 6-speed gearbox is lighter than an 8-speed, twin-clutch automatic one – but the automatic will change gear more quickly. At Lotus, the weight of the car always comes first.

The 360 Cup is really a racing car that you can drive on the road. It is a more luxurious version of the racetrack-only V6 Cup R. The designers did not have a massive challenge to make it more luxurious – the V6 does not even have a passenger seat. The 360 Cup also has air conditioning, and even carpets on (part of) the floor.

Rear spoiler automatically lifts when the car reaches 75 mph

Rear wing and splitter both increase downforce

Side vents channel air to the supercharged engine

The car's control system has four settings: Drive, Sport, Race, and Off (which is only for really brave drivers)

NAME: Colin Chapman
LIVED: 1928–82
FAMOUS AS: Founder of Lotus

Chapman began the Lotus car company in 1952. He once said that, "Adding power makes you faster in a straight line. Subtracting weight makes you faster everywhere." Ever since, Lotus designers have preferred light weight to high power.

Chapman started a Formula 1 team in 1958. His lightweight, mid-engined cars were less powerful than rivals Ferrari and Maserati, but handled much better and used new technology. In the 1960s and 1970s, Lotus won seven Constructors' Championships and six Drivers' Championships.

Price Tag...

For a supercar, this is cheap! Prices start around $83,000 – you could buy six of these instead of a V12 Vantage Zagato, and still have enough money left for a trip to the movies! Unfortunately, though, Lotus only made 50.

What's it like to drive?

Is it quick? Oh Lordy yes … you're fired up the road in double-quick time… It's brilliant.

– review on carmagazine.co.uk

The driver can set the suspension to be softer, to absorb bumps, or harder for racetracks or smooth roads

Front splitter channels air under and through car for maximum downforce

The car interior comes with GRP sports seats, with Lotus stitching, and four-point harnesses as an added extra (where allowed).

WCM 886
GB

TOP SPEED
170 mph
(274 km/h)

0–60 MPH
3.8 seconds

MAX POWER
257 kW
(344 bhp) @ 7,000 rpm

MAX TORQUE
400 Nm
(295 ft/lb) @ 4,500 rpm

 Max RPM:
7,100

 Engine:
3500 cc   supercharged V8

 Weight:
2,480 lbs

 Fuel use per 60 miles:
10.1 liters

 CO2:
235 g/km

 Gearbox:
6-speed manual

 Drive:
rear wheels

 Main body:
fiberglass

 Frame:
aluminum

 Braking:
steel

EXIGE 360 CUP TIMELINE

1996 — Lotus releases the Elise, a mid-engined convertible sports car

2000 — The Exige Series 3 is released, a more powerful car with different bodywork

2012 — The first Exige, based on the Elise, appears

3-ELEVEN

OK, this Lotus is more of a track car than a supercar. But the Lotus 3-Eleven goes 0–60 mph in 2.9 seconds – which is supercar fast. It is supercar impractical, too – it doesn't even have a roof!

Factory: Hethel, Norfolk

WHO NEEDS A WINDSHIELD, ANYWAY?

Speed like the Lotus 3-Eleven's would be exciting in any car. In a car without a windshield, the fun factor is even bigger (unless it starts raining). The driver and passenger wear **full-face helmets**. They are only a little more sheltered from the wind and weather than motorbike racers.

RACE AND ROAD

Lotus makes two versions of the 3-Eleven, the Race and the Road. The Race is more powerful and a bit lighter, but is not really designed for driving on the road. On a racetrack, though, it reaches super-fast speeds. Around the famous **Nürburgring** track, the 3-Eleven is almost as fast as a Porsche 918 Spyder. And in 2016, it actually did a lap of the Hockenheim Grand Prix track FASTER than the 918.

Carbon-fiber rear wing is adjustable on the Race version of the 3-Eleven; fixed in position on the Road version

Roll cage protects driver and passenger if the car turns over in an accident

Large rear wing, plus front and rear splitters, channel air flow to increase performance

LOTUS 3-ELEVEN TIMELINE

1956 — Lotus Eleven, weighing just 900 lbs, is launched; it wins at Le Mans and Sebring

2007 — The 2-Eleven, a doorless open car based on the Lotus Elise, is released

2016 — 3-Eleven available for sale; Lotus plans to make just 311 cars

It will cost you $153,500 for the Race (and $108,700 for the Road). For a car that did a lap of the Nürburgring in 7:06, this is cheap! The fastest car around the course, the Porsche 918 Spyder, is 9 seconds faster — but it costs well over half a million dollars more.

At 150 mph the 3-Eleven Race's aerodynamics create 475 lbs of downforce. That's about the same as having a small bottlenose dolphin lying on the roof.

What's it like to drive?

[The speed is] so vicious and relentless. The initial kick forces the air from your lungs, which is instantly thrust back in [because] you're now doing 100 mph… I'm not sure I've felt acceleration quite like it in any other car I've driven.

– review on *topgear.com*

Splitter draws air in below nose of car

Per 2.2 pounds of weight, the 3-Eleven has almost the same amount of power as a Bugatti Veyron

TOP SPEED
180*mph
(290 km/h)

0–60 MPH
3.0* seconds

MAX POWER
343* kW
(460 bhp) @ 7,000 rpm

MAX TORQUE
525* Nm
(387 ft/lb) @ 3,500 rpm

Max RPM:
7,000+

Engine:
3500 cc supercharged V8

Weight:
2,000 lbs

Fuel use per 60 miles:
est. 10+ liters

CO2:
est. 235 g/km

Gearbox:
6-speed automatic

Drive:
rear wheels

Main body:
carbon

Frame:
aluminum

Braking:
steel

*for 3-Eleven Race (Road: 175 mph, 3.4 sec, 301 kW, 410 Nm)

P1

The F1 was McLaren's first ever supercar and the world's fastest production car. It won the Le Mans 24 Hour race (even though it hadn't been designed for racing) and was regularly voted the greatest car of all time.

Factory: Woking, Surrey

So . . . McLaren had to do something REALLY special for their second supercar.

PARIS, 2012: THE P1 ON SHOW

In 2012, the McLaren stand at the Paris Motor Show was mobbed by car fans. At last, the company was showing the F1's replacement — the long-awaited P1 supercar.

The P1 features layer on layer of Formula 1 technology. Like the Jaguar C-X75, it is a PHEV, using a combination of gas and electric power. The P1's hybrid-power motor is twice as powerful as an F1 car's KERS system. Its aerodynamics adapt to how and where the car is being driven, and it has computer-controlled suspension.

Price Tag...

Good luck — only 375 have been made. All of them were sold within months of the first orders being taken in 2013. (And that was even though prices started at over $1 million.)

P1 V. LAFERRARI V. 918 SPYDER

The P1 only really has two rivals: the Ferrari LaFerrari and the Porsche 918 Spyder. In a test at Britain's Silverstone race circuit, the McLaren came out on top: 0.22 seconds ahead of the Porsche, and 0.34 seconds ahead of the Ferrari.

Roof snorkel sucks air into engine

Custom-made frame with built-in roll cage and door bars for protection

In Race mode, the P1 changes height. It drops 2 inches closer to the ground, and its suspension becomes 300 percent stiffer

Rear wing has a **DRS** feature, which can be opened and closed using a button on the steering wheel

P1 TIMELINE

1992

McLaren F1 is released; 106 cars were
made before production finished in 1998

2012

McLaren P1
is released

NAME: Gordon Murray
LIVED: 1946–present
FAMOUS AS: F1 and McLaren road car designer

Murray worked as a Formula 1 car designer and technical director between
1969 and 2006. He worked at McLaren's Formula 1 team between 1987
and 2006. When the McLaren boss, Ron Dennis, decided the company should
make a fast road car, Murray was put in charge of McLaren Cars. There he helped
produce the F1 and the Mercedes Benz SLR McLaren supercars. He's now helping
to develop a new car for TVR.

What's it like to drive?

*Rest assured, thrill-seeking billionaires … you'd have to have lived a life in
either Top Fuel dragsters or carrier-based fighter planes to grow [used to] this
level of acceleration. It's never terrifying but always scary enough to remind
you what an amazing car it is.*

– review on *caranddriver.com*

The electric motor's power can
be called on by pushing a
button on the steering wheel

*The P1 GTR is a full-on race car version of the P1.
It is more powerful and lighter. If you buy one of
these, McLaren offers you driver training in a
Formula 1* **simulator**!

TOP SPEED

217mph (electronically limite

(350 km/h)

0–60 MPH

28seconds

MAX POWER

675kW

(905 bhp) @ 7,500 rpm

MAX TORQUE

980Nm

(723 lb/ft) @ 7,500 rpm

 Max RPM:
not known

 Engine:
3799 cc   twin-turbo V8 electric motor

 Weight:
3,300 lbs

 Fuel use per 60 miles:
8.3 liters

 CO2:
134 g/km

 Gearbox:
7-speed dual-clutch automatic

 Drive:
rear wheels

 Main body:
carbon fiber

 Frame:
carbon-fiber monocoque

Braking:
carbon-ceramic

650S

This is a supercar you could drive every day. Your mom or dad could use it to drop you at school, or for going to work. They could even head for the gym or the supermarket – the 650S has a big luggage compartment (well, big for a supercar).

So, you could go to the store in it – but why would you? Just starting the engine makes your stomach churn with fear and excitement! The 650S weighs only a bit more than a Lotus Exige 360 Cup, but it has more power than a Porsche 911 GT3. It reaches 60 mph in 3.0 seconds. If you can find somewhere it's allowed, the 650S will reach a top speed of 207 mph.

CARBON MONOCOQUE

At the heart of the 650S is its carbon-fiber monocoque. The rest of the car is built around this structure, which surrounds the driver and passenger. Aluminum frames are attached to the front and rear. These are then used to attach the engine, suspension, and bodywork. The monocoque can be made in just four hours. This is amazing, considering the monocoque for the McLaren F1 (see page 29) took about 4,000 hours to make.

Special doors, typical of McLaren, tilt upward at the rear to let the driver and passenger climb out

Huge side vents channel air into the engine area, keeping it as cool as possible

V8 engine and suspension can be set to Normal, Sport, and Track modes

Magnesium wheels reduce weight by 30 lbs

What's it like to drive?

Holy moly is this car fast. [It accelerates with] the wallop of Thor's hammer, right up to the [8,500] rpm redline… And if the engine is close on perfect then the ride and handling is more than a match.

– review on *telegraph.co.uk*

650S TIMELINE

2011 — McLaren 12C, the first supercar completely designed and built by the company since the F1

2014 — The 650S replaces the 12C; McLaren also releases a convertible version called the 650S Spider

Price Tag...

You can buy one, but only if you have a lot of money. McLaren aims to make about 1,500 of the 650S a year, with the price starting at $257,000.

Aerodynamic, carbon-fiber **mirror stalks** reduce weight and **drag**

Carbon-fiber monocoque weighs just 165 lbs, which is less than an average man

650S

When braking hard from over 60 mph, the air brake at the rear lifts to help slow down the 650S, reducing its stopping distance by up to 65 feet.

McLaren

700 MCL

TOP SPEED

207 mph
(333 km/h)

0–60 MPH

3.0 seconds

MAX POWER

478 kW
(641 bhp) @ 7,250 rpm

MAX TORQUE

678 Nm
(500 ft/lb) @ 6,000 rpm

Max RPM:

8,500

Engine:

3799 cc   twin-turbo V8

Weight:

2,930 lbs

Fuel use per 60 miles:

11.7 liters

CO2:

275 g/km

Gearbox:

7-speed dual-clutch automatic

Drive:

rear wheels

Main body:
carbon fiber

Frame:
carbon-fiber monocoque

Braking:
carbon-ceramic

NOBLE
M600

Noble is a supercar company that does things differently. Other supercar makers keep adding electronic driver aids such as anti-lock brakes, active suspension, and adaptive aerodynamics. Noble refuses to fit almost any of them.

Factory: Leicester, Leicestershire

Roll bars behind seats are made of mixed steel and aluminum

Roll bar for windshield is made of steel

SMALL WEIGHT, BIG POWER

What every M600 does have is light weight (less than a Renault Clio) and huge power (almost twice as much as a Porsche 718 Boxster). Steering an M600 around a racetrack at high speed is a task for skilled drivers only. In fact, this car is so fierce that Noble did have to fit one electronic aid, **traction control**. This can be turned off – but it's not recommended! To stop it happening accidentally, the button is covered with the same flip-up cover used in a Tornado fighter jet.

EVERY CAR A SPECIAL

Each M600 is a "special." Every one is hand built and adapted for the individual customer. Among the options is a "Carbon Sport" body. All M600s have a carbon-fiber body, but the Carbon Sport is not painted. Instead, the carbon fiber is covered in clear, colored lacquer. Noble claims to be the only supercar maker to offer this to its customers.

What's it like to drive?

Raw, brain-mangling performance … not just in a straight line but also around corners, under brakes, during acceleration, everywhere and anywhere. What we are talking about is one of the fastest cars that has ever been built for use on the public road.

– review by autocar.co.uk

Price Tag…

When it was launched in 2009, prices started at $264,000. Many reviewers said they thought this was a bargain price for a car that went as fast as a McLaren F1. By 2016 prices had risen to $330,000 – still a bargain, just not quite such a big one!

223 mph (est.)
(360 km/h)

0–60 MPH

3.0 seconds

MAX POWER

492 kW
(660 bhp) @ 6,500 rpm

MAX TORQUE

819 Nm
(604 ft/lb) @ 3,800 rpm

In 2016, Noble built a prototype M600 Speedster. Instead of a permanent roof, the Speedster had a roof panel that could be removed.

Optional "launch" control button: drivers push this when they want to do the fastest possible start

Max RPM:
7,000

Engine:
4439 cc
V8 twin-turbo

Weight:
2,640 lbs

Fuel use per 60 miles:
11 liters (est.)

CO2:
333 g/km

Gearbox:
6-speed manual

Drive:
rear wheels

Main body:
carbon fiber

Frame:
stainless steel

Braking:
steel

"Comfort" and "sport" mode selector: sport is aimed at racetracks and smooth, fast roads

M600 TIMELINE

2009 — The first M600s are released

2016 — Orders taken for the open-topped M600 Speedster

OTHER BRITISH SUPERCARS

The supercars in this book are some of the newest, fastest, and most exciting supercars made in Britain today. But lots of other fantastic British supercars have been manufactured. Here are a few of them:

MANUFACTURER: ASTON MARTIN
MODEL: ONE-77
YEAR: 2009

First glimpsed in 2008, shown at the Geneva Motor Show in 2009, the One-77 may be the greatest Aston Martin yet. Fitted with a 7300 cc V12 engine, it was voted the most beautiful supercar in several countries. Only 77 were ever made.

MANUFACTURER: BAC
MODEL: MONO
YEAR: 2012

One of the most extreme-looking road cars you will ever see, like a cross between a Formula 1 car and a fighter plane. So fast that, as one reviewer said: "The scenery disappears at a ridiculous rate when you put your foot down."

MANUFACTURER: JAGUAR
MODEL: XJR-15
YEAR: 1990

The world's first production car with a body and chassis made completely of carbon fiber. Only 53 were ever produced; the road version had indicators, bumpers, and a slightly raised body so that it didn't get stuck on speed bumps.

MANUFACTURER: JAGUAR
MODEL: XJ-220
YEAR: 1992

For a brief moment in 1992, the XJ-220 was the coolest (and fastest) British supercar you could buy. Then the McLaren F1 was released, leaving the Jaguar looking a bit old-fashioned. Jaguar planned to make 1,500 but fewer than 300 were built, so the XJ-220 is a very rare car.

MANUFACTURER: MCLAREN
MODEL: F1
YEAR: 1992

Waiting for a plane after the 1988 Italian Grand Prix, four bigwigs from the McLaren Formula 1 team came up with a plan. They would build the best supercar the world had ever seen. It took four years, but when it was released the F1 became the fastest road car the world had ever seen. Only 106 were made.

MANUFACTURER: MCLAREN
MODEL: 12C
YEAR: 2011

The 12C was a long wait for McLaren fans. It was the first production car McLaren had designed and built since it stopped making the F1 in 1998. Fortunately, it was worth the wait. With a 3800 cc V8 engine and a body and frame made mostly of carbon fiber, the 12C can do almost 220 mph.

MANUFACTURER: TVR
MODEL: SAGARIS
YEAR: 2005

They wouldn't be allowed to make this car anymore. TVR thought that safety features, such as **airbags,** made drivers too confident — so they didn't fit any. This is a car that has more power than most drivers can handle.

HISTORICAL BRITISH SUPERCARS

British car makers have always made small, fast 2-seater cars. These were usually called "sporting" or "sports cars." The Jaguar E-Type on pages 4–5 is probably the most famous. Here are just a few of the other historical British supercars.

MANUFACTURER: MG
MODEL: T SERIES
YEAR: 1936

These little two-seat cars had a steel body built on a wooden frame (a technique also used by Morgan). In 1936 they cost the equivalent of about $5,275 in today's money. The MG-TC model became popular in the US after World War II (1939–45). American soldiers liked the cars, which were not like anything you could buy in the US.

MANUFACTURER: JAGUAR
MODEL: XK-120
YEAR: 1949

The "120" stood for 120 mph, which was the speed the XK-120 could reach. That may not sound supercar fast today – but back in 1949, it made the Jag the fastest road car you could buy.

MANUFACTURER: AUSTIN HEALEY
MODEL: 3000
YEAR: 1959

The 3000 managed to squeeze 115 mph out of its 2912 cc inline-6 engine – and it was so low to the ground that it felt a lot faster. The car raced (and won) at circuits around the world. When the Mini Cooper S appeared in 1963, the 3000 became less popular as a racing car.

MANUFACTURER: LOTUS
MODEL: ELAN
YEAR: 1962

The Elan was a tiny little sports car with a steel frame and a fiberglass body. It was famous for its excellent handling. When Gordon Murray finished the McLaren F1 design (see page 23), he apparently said he only had one disappointment. It was that the F1 didn't steer as well as a Lotus Elan.

MANUFACTURER: MORGAN
MODEL: PLUS 8
YEAR: 1968

Showing that some drivers like nothing more than some REALLY old-fashioned fun, the Plus 8 only stopped production in 2004. (One of Morgan's current designs, the 3-Wheeler, is descended from a car that was first made in 1911.)

30

GLOSSARY

aerodynamics how air flows around an object

airbag balloon that inflates when a car is in an accident, cushioning the driver or passengers

bodywork the outer shell of a vehicle

bhp short for brake horsepower, an alternative unit of power to kW

bucket seat seat with a rounded back that fits around your sides, holding you in place when going round a corner at high speed

chassis frame

coachworks maker of specialist car parts, particularly the outside panels

downforce downward pressure on the tires, which makes them grip the road better

drag air resistance

DRS short for Drag Reduction System, which controls the angle of a car's rear wing to increase top speed

full-face helmet crash helmet that covers your whole head and face, right down to your chin

inline 6 engine with 6 cylinders in a row; Jaguar's inline 6 was in development since 1947

KERS short for Kinetic Energy Recovery System, a way of storing a car's braking force

manual gears a driver has to change for herself, using a gearstick

mirror stalk part that attaches a side-view mirror to a vehicle

monocoque object that gets its strength from its outer layer, instead of a supporting frame or skeleton

petrolhead a British term meaning a fan of anything fast and gas-powered, but especially cars

Nürburgring famous racetrack in Germany, made partly of normal roads, where many supercar makers go to test their cars

simulator machine that is designed to allow you to practice for a real-world dangerous situation in a safe way

splitter feature that controls air flow at the front or rear of a car, usually as a way of improving downforce

spoiler wing at the back of a car that presses downward as air flows over it, improving the tires' grip

stop-start system computer-controlled system for stopping a car when it is not moving, then restarting it again when the driver wants to move off. Stop-start systems are a way of saving fuel and causing less pollution.

supercharger device for feeding extra air into an engine, which increases its power. A supercharger has the same effect as a turbocharger, but is powered in a different way.

synchromesh gearbox technology that helps the driver move forward smoothly after putting the car into a new gear

torque the amount of "work" exerted by an engine

traction control system for stopping a car's tires losing grip

tricked out fully accessorized, with lots of non-factory upgrades

wing another word for a spoiler

INDEX

FURTHER INFORMATION

Books

Crum, Colin. *Porsche vs. Lotus*. New York, NY: Windmill Books, 2014.

Goldsworthy, Steve. *Scorching Supercars*. North Mankato, MN: Capstone Press, 2015.

Phillips, Adam. *Supercars*. New York, NY: Rosen Publishing, 2013.

Website

PowerKids Press has developed an online list of websites related to the subject of this book. This site is updated regularly. Please use this link to access the list: www.powerkidslinks.com/sc/british